BOOK FOUR

The fight against racism

THE INSTITUTE OF RACE RELATIONS
2-6 Leeke Street, London WC1X 9HS, England

© Institute of Race Relations 1986
ISBN 0 85001 031 4

Cover photo (bottom) by G.M. Cookson
Designed by Hilary Arnott
Typeset by Boldface, 17a Clerkenwell Road, London EC1
Printed by the Russell Press (TU), Gamble Street, Nottingham
Published and distributed by the Institute of Race Relations

CONTENTS

PREFACE

This is the fourth in our series of anti-racist educational books for young people – a series which was initially prompted by our realisation that the propagation and development of multi-cultural education did nothing to tackle the fundamental issue of racism.

We had pointed out to the Rampton (subsequently Swann) Committee that 'while multicultural studies may, in explaining differences in customs and cultures, help to modify attitudes, such studies are primarily an extension of existing educational techniques and methods, and, as such, allow racism within society, and within the educational system, to pass unchallenged. And education itself comes to be seen in terms of an adjustment process within a racist society and not as a force for changing the values that make that society racist...Just to learn about other people's cultures is not to learn about the racism of one's own. To learn about the racism of one's own culture, on the other hand, is to approach other cultures objectively'.

Our first book in the series, *Roots of racism*, looked at the historical origins of racism generally; the second, *Patterns of racism*, at the way that racism was shaped and formed in different countries at different periods of time; the third, a cartoon book, *How racism came to Britain*, looked specifically at the way racism had worked itself into the very structures and institutions of British society. Here, in *The fight against racism*, we attempt to show, in words and pictures, how Asian and Afro-Caribbean peoples have resisted and organised against such racism since the Second World War – creating at different times and in differing areas new forms and traditions of struggle in Britain.

This pictorial history includes key images from the exhibition 'From resistance to rebellion' which is a useful companion to the present book and available for hire from the Institute of Race Relations. Black history, we believe, should not be restricted to information about the countries from which black people came, or to the lives of a few black heroes or heroines. Black history has been made here, in Britain, by whole communities – it is a history which needs to be recognised both on its own account and as a contribution to the history of working people generally. *The fight against racism* will, we hope, help young people, both black and white, to appreciate the richness of that history, and understand current issues in its light. Since the book covers such new and little known territory, some suggestions for further reading are provided.

A. Sivanandan
Director
Institute of Race Relations

INTRODUCTION

The resistance of black people to racism in Britain was formed by their struggles against slavery and colonialism. For over 300 years, Britain (like other colonising powers such as Portugal, Holland and France) had controlled and exploited black countries and was unwilling to give up its profitable domination. Black people had therefore to fight this

through revolutionary ideas

Marcus Garvey was the founder in the early twentieth century of a mass movement (the United Negro Improvement Association) which spread ideas of black dignity and self-reliance in the USA, Caribbean and Africa.

through mass agitation

Mahatma Gandhi, who inspired a mass liberation movement in India through satyagraha (passive resistance to oppression), on the Salt March of 1930.

through armed struggle.

The Land and Freedom Army of Kenya (Mau Mau) which fought British colonialism in the 1950s.

ARRIVAL

During the Second World War, which Britain fought against Germany, many black soldiers from Britain's colonies all over the world fought and died to support its cause.

THE SPACIOUS - COMFORTABLE - LUXURIOUS -

"Santa Maria"

SAILS **AUGUST 26th!**

BOOK NOW FOR **ENGLAND**

via VIGO, SPAIN
FROM WHICH PORT PASSENGERS
WILL BE TRANSPORTED BY TRAIN
TO LONDON, ENGLAND at NO
EXTRA COST!

KINGSTON TO LONDON
FOR ONLY
£75

SEE YOUR TRAVEL AGENT IMMEDIATELY!

H. MACAULAY ORRETT LTD. 507 KING ST. KINGSTON

GENERAL AGENTS FOR: COMPANHIA COLONIAL DE NAVEGAÇAO

After the war, which had killed off so many people, Britain was desperate for workers to operate the factories, run the hospitals and maintain transport and other services. In 1948 the Government passed a Nationality Act making all colonial and Commonwealth citizens British and actively recruited black people (left workless in their countries through centuries of colonial rule) to come to Britain to fill the unpopular and dirty jobs.

Tom Blau/Camera Press

Black people were wanted for their labour, resented for their presence.

A 'colour bar' operated to keep them in the worst jobs, the worst housing and the worst areas, and out of clubs, churches, pubs and dance halls.

RGANISING SELF-RELIANCE

ring the 1950s black people set up their own clubs, welfare and cultural associations
l religious institutions and organised their own ways of beating the 'colour bar'.

A network of Indian
Workers' Associations was
soon flourishing.

A host of West Indian
organisations sprang up.
They took their inspiration
from the League of Coloured
Peoples (founded in 1931)
and the Pan-African
Federation, whose fifth
Congress, held in
Manchester in 1945, attracted
key black anti-colonial
fighters such as Nkrumah,
Kenyatta, Padmore, James
and Du Bois.

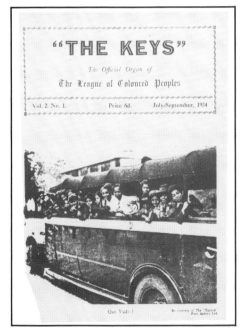

Hulton Picture Library

When, by the end of the 1950s, the post-war boom was over and the need for black labour decreased, the call by racists for immigration control found an economic 'excuse'. The pre-war fascist parties joined with the right wing of the Tory Party to claim the need for 'racial preservation', and racial attacks, which were already known in Cardiff and Liverpool, became a feature of black life.

CARDIFF TIMES AND SOUTH WALES WEEKLY NEWS.

SATURDAY. AUGUST 9. 1919.

FATAL SHOT.

ALLEGED MURDER

In Cardiff Negro-Land.

DEATH OF A SOMALI.

Maria-street, off Bute-road, Cardiff, was the scene of an alleged murder at 9.10 on Sunday night.

Crowds of coloured men had gathered in the street all through the day, and various tribes of Arabs and Somalis appeared to be on the best of terms. Towards 9.30 p.m. the jesting by a number of the tribe of Aberjarols caused a Somali of the name of Hassan ... to produce a revolver.

Immediately prior to the shooting there had been an altercation between two Somalis, one of whom sustained an injury to the left eye. Then ensued a row between four coloured men, and the shooting followed.

There was pandemonium for a time, and hosts of residents from both rows of houses came into the street.

Mrs Shay, a boarding-house-keeper, said she was in the front room of No. 12, Maria-street, when she heard two shots. She thought there were fireworks, and went to the door, and was startled to see the deceased man stagger against the wall. She went towards him, and his companions carried him dying into Mrs Shay's house. Mrs Shay ...

LIVERPOOL ECHO, AUGUST 17, 1948

"Baton Practice" Denial By Liverpool Police

CHALLENGE IN RIOT CASE

Running Fight Described

NIGHT SCENES

Evidence Of Men's Injuries Disputed

Cases arising out of the racial disturbances in Liverpool on the nights of August 1 and 2 were heard by the Liverpool Deputy Stipendiary Magistrate (Mr. A. F. Baucher), at a special court to-day.

Fifty-four persons were accused, and the great majority coloured men, and the proceedings are expected to last several days.

Mr. J. R. Bishop, who prosecuted, said that arising out of the racial incidents there were altogether some 70 defendants. He understood that Mr Harry Livermore represented 40 defendants.

It seemed that on August 2, as on two previous nights, there had been some kind of disturbances in the Upper Parliament Street section of the city and there were a number of streets...

"that the trouble was about. I don't think I need go into," said Mr Bishop. "It appears to have...

THE TIMES

FRIDAY SEPTEMBER 12 1958

NOTTINGHAM COLOURED PEOPL "WILL BE ATTACKED AGAIN"

MR. MANLEY HEARS OF ALLEGED THREA

From Our Correspondent

...HAM, Sept. 11

...ey, Chief Minister ...y coloured people ...agham's coloured ...there had been

later lead to racial strife. But, just a a great challenge to Britain to solve prejudices which exist, so it is a challer you to bring to bear on the problem patience and understanding that we built up in the Caribbean area over ...

Paddington Mercury

MIDDLESEX INDEPENDENT & WEST LONDON STAR

3, GEORGE ST., BAKER ST., W.1.
(Adjacent Marylebone High Street) WELbeck 2870.

201, HIGH STREET, N.W.10.
ELGar 6192.

6357   FRIDAY. SEPTEMBER 12. 1958   THREEPENCE

GANGS TERRORISE NEGROES

Churches ask governments to take action in race clashes

RENEWED RACIAL VIOLENCE FLARED IN PADDINGTON OVER THE WEEK-END ON SATURDAY RIOTERS BATTLED WITH SCORES OF POLICE IN THE HARROW ROAD AS THE MOBS WERE ANGRY THAT THEIR COLOURED PREY HAD STAYED INDOORS.

A petrol bomb was thrown into a house in Brindley Road, Paddington, on Sunday night. Four people were taken to hospital.

And on Monday, seven local clergymen appealed to the Government to make a full inquiry. They urged the "reconciliation of conflicting groups."

A team of "Mercury" reporters who ran to the scene found ...toured the borough seeking ...one there. All the windows ...ing signs of racial violence at "The Gardens" ...

Evening Gazette

No 29,314   91st Year   MONDAY, AUGUST 21, 1961   M2   Price 5d

Full story of Cannon-street disturbances unfolded

35 MEN; ONE WOMAN FACE

AFTER THE STORM ...

BORO' COURT

An array of bandages

...EEKEND violence and hooliganism involving literally ...housands of people—as Det.-Insp. John Dennison ...ribed it—resulted in the appearance in Middlesbrough ...istrates' Court today of 35 men and one woman.

Middlesbrough's packed main courtroom was reserved for the ...ng.

...andaged arms, heads and hands could be seen both among the ranks ...r police officers, and among the accused men as they filed in groups ...he well of the court.

A total of 13 policemen and about seven civilians were treated at Middlesbrough ...ral Hospital during the weekend after disturbances in Cannon-street boundary ...t and Bridge-street.

...x policemen were still detained in hospital today, but most because of this arose of ...y would not go out.

Disturbances started in Cannon-street on Saturday ...night after public house closing time, broke out again in ...Boundary-road yesterday afternoon, and were repeated ...in a side area near the town centre last night.

Three people fined

The Stipendiary Magistrate (Mr A. P. Prasher) had heard about 30 cases by lunchtime, and postponed sentence on the majority until later in the day.

When the court adjourned, the charges against five people remained to be tried. 18 realised sentence, four had been remanded in custody, three had been fined, two had been given conditional discharges, and four juveniles had been remitted to the juvenile court.

Express & Star

AND BIRMINGHAM EVENING EXPRESS

TOWN

Phone: W'hampton 22233; Want Ads 26641   Monday, August 16, 1965   No. 28172, Price Fourpence

A troubled weekend in Wolverhampton...

4 NIGHTS WORTH FORGETTING

'Keep cool' plea by racial harmonists

RACE hatred has brought four nights of pandemonium to Wolverhampton's Low Hill council housing estate.

Since Thursday closing time at public houses in the district has signalled the start of squabbles between white and coloured people which threatened, at times, to flare up into a large-scale race riot.

A man who said he was prepared to follow anyone in "a fight with the blacks" just about summed up the attitude of large crowds who gathered on Saturday night and last night in the Broome-road area—scene of a bottle and brick attack by about 150 white people on some Jamaicans on Friday night.

The crowds were just waiting for someone to start something.

And when scuffles did break out between Jamaicans and ...

for some time, until a man refused to move as police were trying to clear Broome-road. He was warned that he was committing an offence and that he might be arrested.

After being given a short time to change his mind, he still refused to move. He was taken to a police car, but then his father intervened and managed to persuade him to return home.

Later Broome-road looked almost clear, but there were still hundreds of people in the adjacent streets.

Suddenly there came a chorus of shouts and cries from women in nearby Fifth avenue. Immediately the crowds went rushing down there, including many who materialised from out of the gloom in Broome-road.

It appeared that a scuffle had started, but the police were extremely fast in getting it stopped. They cleared the crowds away once more, and slowly attention drifted back to Broome-road.

Among the police vehicles was ...

On Sunday evening the mood was equally ugly. At closing time, the Corner House Inn was again the focal point of disturbances, and police intervened two men in connection with allegations of carrying offensive weapons early in the evening.

Large crowds again gathered on the public house car park and in the road. They were all white.

A few West Indians walked past, and police stepped between them and some of the crowd which moved to follow.

At one point several West Indians were jeered at by the gathering, and shortly after this an incident involving a number of white women occurred.

For a time there was chaos in the road as pedestrians blocked the way of traffic. Then police started to move away the crowds once more, and were successful in getting everyone away by around midnight.

During the evening Press cameramen were jostled as they tried to take photographs.

The weekend racial trouble in Wolverhampton has brought appeals for calm from leading campaigners for racial harmony in the Midlands.

Miss Shirley Fostick, secretary of the Birmingham co-ordinating committee against racial discrimination, told the Express and Star today: "With the violence and death currently occurring in America, many people must fear that the incidents in Wolverhampton may lead to further violence and destruction here in Britain.

"The recent Government White Paper on immigration has unfortunately created an atmosphere in which racialism, resulting in such incidents, has been encouraged.

"The committee calls upon all responsible organisations and individuals to take whatever action they can to ensure that such an incident does not occur again."

"KEEP COOL"

A plea for both white and coloured people to "keep cool" ...

Ayr ... liaison officer for the West Midland Commonwealth Welfare Council.

"I hope that they will not do anything to inflame the position," he added, "but will only try to work and speak constructively."

Mr. Ayre said that while he very much deplored the trouble, it was obviously a police matter at the moment, and he would wait a while before seeing if he could take any action.

The trouble at Bushbury is more of a domestic matter than that which caused trouble in Dudley a few years ago, said Superintendent H. Williams, Deputy Chief Constable of Wolverhampton, today.

The two issues also differed in that the Bushbury one was confined to a small area of the town, he said.

He also mentioned that he wished that Press cameramen would not go near to the scenes at night. "I don't think they help the situation," he said.

He concluded: "I would hope that the situation there will settle down and become quiet soon, and that there will be no more disturb-...

DAILY HERALD

No. 13219 (C) Tuesday, September 2 1958 Price 2½d

Petrol bomb thrown as 200 surround house
RACE WAR SIEGE

Forty arrested as police, with dogs, swoop at midnight

MEN WITH KNIVES ROUNDED UP

By HERALD REPORTING TEAM:
Denis Pitts. Maurice Fagence.
Brian Woosey. John Mason

FORTY terrified Jamaicans barricaded themselves in their home last night – the second night of London's race war – and hit back at the me[...] agers who held them in[...]

The coloured men hurled b[...] of the house in Blenheim-cr[...] and a petrol bomb was also i[...]

At midnight, two special Bra[...] with crowbars forced their way i[...] were taken away

Altogether 40 people were arr[...] half white –and Black Marias t[...]

RACIAL FIGHTS IN LONDON

PATROLLING CARS STONED

MIDNIGHT ARRESTS

More than 400 people were involved in disturbances last night at Notting Hill Gate, London, where police were still patrolling in pairs, after fighting between white and coloured people on Saturday night.

Soon after midnight 18 persons, four of them coloured, had been arrested and charged. Eight of the 18 were charged with using insulting behaviour, two with assaulting police, and three with possessing offensive weapons. They will appear at West London court later to-day.

In August 1958 large-scale 'riots' broke out when Mosleyites and the White Defence League declared war on Notting Hill's black residents.

Popperfoto

The blacks struck back.

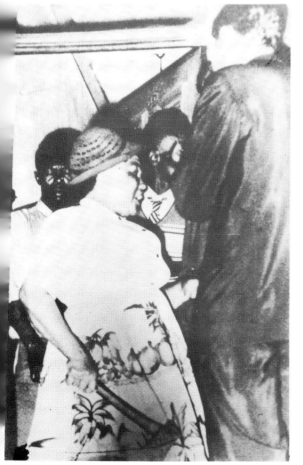

"You know, they were going to fight to the death; there were women cutting up sheets and bandages, they had the whole roofs sorted out, and they decided that they weren't going to have no more of it."

(Struggles for black community, 1983)

Ken Sprague/Searchlight

A West Indian carpenter, Kelso Cochrane, was stabbed to death on the streets of Notting Hill in London. Police failed to find the killer – the first of many such failures.

The funeral procession turned into a mass demonstration, as it was to do again and again at the funerals of

Satnam Singh Gill in Coventry (1981)

Mike Abrahams/Network

Michael Ferreira in Hackney (1979)

G.M. Cookson

Andrew Wiard/Report

and of thirteen young people burned to death at a Deptford party (1981).

IGHTING DISCRIMINATION

The racial violence of 1958 impressed on the West Indian community the need for greater organisation.

Claudia Jones launched the *West Indian Gazette* (the first Afro-Asian paper).

In 1959, Claudia, together with Frances Ezzreco, led a deputation of black organisations to the Home Secretary.

BRUMMIES UNITE TO FIGHT MIGRANTS BAN

Now, with immigration controls in the offing, other organisations began to develop – the West Indian Standing Conference, the Pakistani Workers' Association, the West Indian Workers' Association – which united with others to form umbrella organisations to campaign against racist immigration laws.

Claudia Jones and A. Manchanda speaking at a Hyde Park rally against the immigration bill.

The Commonwealth Immigrants Act was passed in 1962, and, by implying that black British citizens were not really citizens and should be kept out of the country, it institutionalised racism in the law of the land.

In the workplace the Act gave a boost to trade union racism, which, combined with poor pay, bad conditions and no job security, made the position of black workers intolerable.

The workers struck – at Courtaulds Red Scar Mill, Preston, at Woolfs rubber factory, Hayes, at Coneygre Foundry, Tipton, at Birmid Qualcast.

And because the unions would not help them, they looked to their own communities and organisations for support, developing in the process their own methods of struggle.

Indians and Pakistanis crowd the Crossed Guns pub in West Bromwich for a strike meeting.

In society at large the Act made racism respectable. The 'colour bar' of the 1950s was now becoming blatant and entrenched. It had to be fought in firms where whites refused to work alongside blacks, in pubs which would not serve blacks and in official policy.

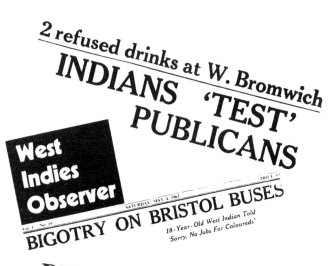

2 refused drinks at W. Bromwich

INDIANS 'TEST' PUBLICANS

West Indies Observer

Vol. 1 No. 19   SATURDAY, MAY 4, 1963   PRICE 3d

BIGOTRY ON BRISTOL BUSES

18-Year-Old West Indian Told 'Sorry, No Jobs For Coloureds'

DEPUTATION MOVE OVER 'COLOUR BAR'

𝕶𝖊𝖓𝖘𝖎𝖓𝖌𝖙𝖔𝖓 𝕻𝖔𝖘𝖙

TENANTS TOLD: 'GET RID OF RELATIVES LIVING WITH YOU'

Martin Luther King, the black American civil rights worker who mounted a mass campaign against the segregation of blacks in the USA, visited London in 1964 and encouraged Asians and West Indians to join together into a national Campaign Against Racial Discrimination (CARD).

Claudia Jones with Martin Luther King at Africa Unity House in 1961.

CARD

Campaign Against Racial Discrimination

CAMPAIGN

the newsletter of CARD   N°2   1/-

IMMIGRANTS CALL FOR LAWS

C. A. R. D.

HOW TO EXPOSE

DISCRIMINATIO

Issued by the CAMPAIGN AGAINST RACIAL DISCRIMIN,
23 St.George's House,Tavma Hill,
Commercial Street,London.E.1.
Tel: BIS-5751.

AIMS AND OBJECTIVES

1.   To struggle for the elimination of all racial discrimination against coloured people in the United Kingdom.

2.   To struggle for the elimination of all forms of discrimination against minority groups in the United Kingdom.

3.   To use all means in our power to combat racial prejudice.

4.   To oppose all forms of discrimination on the entry of Commonwealth citizens into the United Kingdom.

5.   To oppose all legislation that is racially discriminatory or inspired by racial prejudice.

6.   (a) To seek to co-ordinate the work of organisations already in the field, and to act as a clearing house for information about the fight against discrimination in Britain.

      (b) To establish and maintain links with organisations outside the United Kingdom having aims and objects broadly similar to those of CARD.

BLACK POWER

MAGNET

Magnet News No. 2. February 27—March 12, 1965. Price 6d.

THE VOICE OF THE AFRO-ASIAN CARIBBEAN PEOPLES

MALCOLM X
TRAGEDY OF THE AMERICAN SOCIETY

In London when Jimmy Baldwin, the Afro-American novelist, heard of the death of Malcolm X he declared, " This is an act which has sprung from the moral climate of America. . . . And that climate has tolerated uncounted negro deaths—the killing of children . . .

By the mid-60s the civil rights movement in America was giving way to Black Power and it sounded a chord among Britain's radical blacks.

RAAS
KNOWS
HOW TO GET—

—*a voice in your union*
better working conditions —
—*promotion on the job*
decent housing —
—*education*
opportunity —
—*full equality*
WE CAN TELL YOU

Taking their cue from Malcolm X, a powerful figure in the USA, activists set up a militant black mass movement called the Racial Action Adjustment Society which worked to improve the living and working conditions for blacks.

The United Coloured People's Association, which stressed the international dimension of black power, is here being addressed by US Black Power leader Stokely Carmichael.

BLACK POWER SPEAKS

FIRST ISSUE · JUNE 1968

PRICE 2'-

Black Power Speaks

Produced by
P.P.P.

U.C.P.A.
fully support the Irish people
in their just struggle for
self-determination.
* * * * * * * * * * * * * * *

nce again British imperialism has murdered sons of Ireland so that
ey may continue to exploit the Irish people.
are confident that the Irish people, under correct revolutionary
dership, will rise up save upon wave, and deal a stinging blow to
barbarious imperialist system which has oppressed and exploited
for so long   *****

RK, 2.00 p.m.

LE !

S.W.2.

Black power is black unity

BLACK POWER IS BLACK UNITY

"Unity is strength". Black people, (that is, Africans,
West Indians, Indians, Pakistanis, Chinese, Arabs and all
non-white peoples), united together can and will gain their
human rights. We, the black people, need the unity which
Black Power. But we must first understand ourselves. BE
BLACK IS NOT HOW DARK OR LIGHT YOUR SKIN IS BECAUSE, IF
NOT WHITE, YOU ARE CONSIDERED BLACK. Therefore brothers
sisters we must have black unity now.

BLACK CONSCIOUSNESS

Before we can have Black Unity and Black Power, we m'
be conscious of what we have in common. We must be a
common problems. We must be aware of our common opp?
We must be aware of the common enemy. But we cannot
talking forever about unity; we must do something :
We have to bury our differences and get our heads

We must recognize our blackness and realize that '
discriminated against simply because we are black
blackness which joins us together, we must accept'
accepting ourselves as we are and wear our blac'
When we realize that we are all in the same boat
join together to solve our common problem.

Support the Afro-American
struggle against fascism in
the U.S.A.

Picket U.S. Embassy
Grosvenor Sq.

FRIDAY.......18th JULY, 1969 . FROM IO A.M. TO 6 P.M.
SATURDAY.....19th JULY, 1969 . FROM IO A.M. TO 4 P.M.

****

FORGING BLACK UNITY

1968 was to prove a watershed. The Labour Government decided in March to bar entry into Britain of its citizens from Kenya, because they were Asian. Tory politician Enoch Powell stoked the racist fires with inflammatory speeches and the press picked up Powell's theme.

BRITAIN MUST BE MAD, LITERALLY MAD—ENOCH

It's like watching a nation heaping up its funeral pyre

Enoch Powell, a "Shadow" Minister and one of the MPs for immigrant-packed Wolverhampton, dropped a racial bombshell today in a speech at Birmingham. "Britain," he declared, "must be mad, literally mad as a nation, to be permitting the annual inflow of some 50,000 wives and children of immigrants already here."

MR. ENOCH POWELL

Like the Roman —I seem to see the river of blood

HOME NEWS

Mosley speeches recalled

Powell figures 'fantasy'

There was strong reaction during the weekend to Mr Powell's controversial views on immigrants...

"The unspeakable had been spoken, racism set free: Asians and West Indians were attacked and abused, their property damaged. Police harassment increased, the fascists went on a rampage and Paki-bashing emerged as a national sport."

(A. Sivanandan)

CLUB REAFFIRMS COLOUR BAR

FROM OUR CORRESPONDENT—Wolverhampton, April 21

Seven hundred members of a Midlands working men's club today agreed unanimously to continue a 10-year-old colour bar. The rule forbids coloured visitors and entertainers to enter the North Wolverhampton Working Men's Club in Oxley Street, Wolverhampton.

Members, who voted by a show of hands, gave the decision a standing ovation. The ballot...

'Incitement to racial hatred'

Defending his speech yesterday on the B.B.C. radio programme *The World this Weekend*, Mr. Powell said: "I spoke about the deep fears, the resentments and anxieties for the future which I know exist."

Mr Powell filled with foreboding on immigrants

In his speech on immigration and the Government's Race Relations Bill Mr. Enoch Powell, Conservative M.P. for Wolverhampton, South-West, said that as he looked ahead he was filled with foreboding. "Like the Roman, I seem to see the river Tiber foaming with much blood."

He went on: "That tragic and intractable phenomenon which we watch with horror on the other side of the Atlantic but which there is interwoven with the history and existence of the states itself, is coming upon us here by our own volition and our own neglect.

"Indeed, it has all but come in numerical terms, it will be of American proportions long before the end of the century. Only resolute and urgent action will avert it even now.

"Whether there will be the public will to demand and obtain that..."

Popperfoto

As dockers marched in support of Powell, representatives from over 50 black organisations (including RAAS, UCPA, WISC and IWA) came together to form the Black People's Alliance.

Their march on Downing Street attracted over 7,000 people.

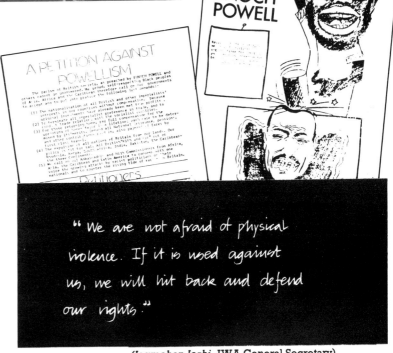

" We are not afraid of physical violence. If it is used against us, we will hit back and defend our rights."

(Jagmohan Joshi, IWA General Secretary)

Stefano Cagnoni/IFL

Protest outside US embassy after the invasion of Grenada, 1983.

Protesting against Mrs Gandhi's Emergency of 1975-1977

Gertrude Elias Collection

Protest outside Portuguese embassy, 1965.

Fighting racism in Britain inevitably extended to fighting repression elsewhere.

Lance Watson

Protest outside South Africa House after shooting of children in Soweto, 1976.

From **BPA** and the Black Power movement sprang a host of organisations, parties and papers to serve black communities up and down the country.

HUNDREDS DEPORTED SECRETLY EVERY WEEK

Soledad Brothers 'Not Guilty'

PETROL BOMB ATTACK

BLACK VOICE PAGE 2

BLACK UNITY AND FREEDOM PARTY MANIFESTO

LONG TERM PROGRAMME

SHORT TERM AIMS

BRADFORD BLACK

JAMAICAN MURDERED BY RACISTS

BLACK CHAT

FREEDOM NEWS

ANGELA DAVIS VICTORY DAY

Metro 4 Acquitted!!

BLACK STRUGGLE

a fight for dignity

JANATA'S MISERIES see inside

NATIONAL CONFERENCE

STRUGGLE FOR OUR HUMAN RIGHTS

22-23 MAY 1971

ALEXANDRA PALACE - LONDON - 22.

TriContinental outpost

PEOPLE'S DEMANDS

1 We demand, full employment for all black people living in the United Kingdom.

2 We demand, better housing conditions for all black people and a voice in the re-allocation of houses for our people.

3 We demand an end to police brutality and the persecution of our leaders.

4 We demand freedom for all black people in prison.

5 We demand that all black people be tried by their own Peer Group as is written in the Magna Carta.

6 We demand education for our people that expose the true nature of this racist society.

BLACK DIMENSION April 1969
Vol 1 / 3

Forging black unity / 19

Black groups hosted meetings for black figures whose struggles, ideas and writings had inspired the British black movement.

Amilcar Cabral, one of the greatest revolutionary leaders of the twentieth century and founder of the African Independence Party of Guiné and Cape Verde (PAIGC), talked in 1971 to packed audiences at Central Hall, Westminster, and Manchester Town Hall. (He was assassinated two years later.)

Patrick Eager/Report

Mme Nguyen Thi Binh was the representative at the Paris Peace talks of the Provisional Revolutionary Government of South Vietnam. In 1969 she spoke in London at a Vietnam anti-war rally.

Lance Watson

Angela Davis, the FBI's 'Most wanted woman in America', was imprisoned in the 1970s for her activities in the Black Power movement. Agitation for her release extended to Britain, which she visited shortly after being released in 1976.

Lance Watson

Walter Rodney, activist and founder of the Guyanese Working People's Alliance, was banned from Jamaica in 1968, from taking up a post at the University of Guyana in 1974, and murdered by pro-government forces in 1983.

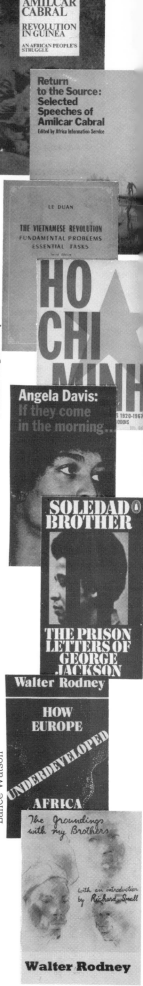

BUILDING BLACK COMMUNITY

fro-Caribbeans and Asians began to fight as a class and as a people; the experience of a ommon racism and a common fight against the state united them, so that, by the beginning f the 1970s, black became the colour of one's politics, not the colour of one's skin.

Basing themselves in the poorest black areas, groups put their expertise and ideas at the service of local needs.

Black People's Information Centre, Notting Hill

Meals at the Black House, London, 1970.

Asian Resource Centre, Handsworth.

FLAMINGO

Published by

CHALTON PUBLISHING CO. LTD.
2-4 LUDGATE CIRCUS BUILDINGS
LONDON, E.C.4.   Tel.: CENtral 1732

Volume 4, No. 9

THE PARDNER SYSTEM

THIS is the story of a revolution which will hardly hit the headlines. The people who lead it have no desire to change anything or overthrow any institution. They are West Indians operating a traditional form of monetary savings which is based on individual trust.

In a very quiet way an informal circle of people referred to as bankers and controlling the well-known West Indian banking system known as Pardner, Box or Sou-Sou—the different label is applied according to the part of the Caribbean the persons come from—are at the centre of an economic phenomenon among West Indians in Britain. In the absence of written record of the background and history of the Pardner system in the West Indies, I undertook an investigation of the basic mechanism of this method of thrift in Jamaica a few years ago and it was used as the basis for a report which appeared in the "Welfare Reporter".

It was then found to be most popular among people who earned regular or irregular incomes which were merely enough to take care of bare necessities. In its form, the system is closely related to the Chinese fui practice, which contains an element of speculation not very far removed from the intricacies of a stock exchange.

It starts off like this: there might be a small gathering of friends—about ten—in a home. This meeting might even take place among co-workers at a factory. After having quenched their thirst with some sort of beverage or spirit and after having discussed many subjects, one of them will put forward the suggestion that "it would be helpful to us if we were to have a Pardner". His suggestion is unanimously accepted. They next agree that their individual weekly contribution will be a set £5. They now turn to the appointment of the banker, the man in charge, to whom each "will throw", to use the vernacular, his weekly contribution, and from whom each will receive alternately a "weekly draw" of £50.

Now one of the most commendable features of this banking system is that it dismisses the mass of paper work which is carried out in the orthodox banking system. The only stationery that the banker will have in his possession will be a diary or exercise book with a pen or pencil to set down the names of those in the Pa there are ten persons in it will run for ten weeks,

It was around housing that both Asians and Afro-Caribbeans had first organised. Facing discrimination in the private and public rented sectors, they developed their own ways of housing their community by, for instance, pooling money in a mortgage club within a group (the Pardner system).

In the 1970s, the fight extended to protecting whole communities against the developer, and councils' attempts to relegate blacks to inferior estates.

In the 1980s, it meant fighting against homelessness.

Bengali families took over Camden Town Hall in 1984 after a mother and two children were burned to death in the temporary bed-and-breakfast accommodation provided by the Council.

The education of black children was a priority. **Asian children** were being bussed to schools outside their areas from 1965.

Colin Davey/Camera Press

DEMO AGAINST 'BUSSING' PLANNED

'Build schools and stop the bussing' demo

Schools dispersal is attacked as apartheid

The community resisted, set up Saturday schools, and fought against racist teaching.

BERNARD COARD

HOW THE WEST INDIAN CHILD
IS MADE EDUCATIONALLY SUB-NORMAL
IN THE BRITISH SCHOOL SYSTEM

Afro-Caribbean children were being
relegated to educationally subnormal schools.
Black parents fought this mis-education and
helped to set up supplementary schools.

The content of education
denied the black experience
of racism and colonialism;
'black studies' provided an
alternative.

When black children were
deemed 'disruptive', it was
black teachers and parents,
again, who organised
against this.

Community defence campaigns for those arrested and/or framed by the police became a permanent feature of black politics.

Clubs were raided, black events harassed. The youth fought back – at the Mangrove in 1970, the Metro in 1971, Brockwell Park Fair in 1973, the Carib Club in 1974, Chapeltown Bonfire Night in 1975.

Andrew Wiard/Report

Schoolboy Cliff McDaniel was arrested outside his school in 1973.

1 October 1971

JUSTICE FOR THE MANGROVE 9

Police Attack Notting Hill Demo August 1970

9 Black People Appear At Old Bailey OCTOBER 4 1971

We Demand To Be Tried by Black Jurors

Paddington Mercury

MANY HURT IN METRO YOUTH CLUB BATTLE

BRADFORD BLACK

Bonfire Night Belongs To Us

DEFEND THE 7 MOZART WOMEN

SEVEN BLACK WOMEN BEATEN UP IN THEIR OWN HOME ON MOZART ESTATE AND

BLACK AND BLUE IN BURNGREAVE

FRONT LINES

John Sturrock/Network

The Knight family were harassed and beaten up by the police after being racially abused by their neighbours in 1983.

Chris Davies/Report

The community picketed Harlesden police station where six girls were beaten up by police in 1976.

FREEDOM FOR BLACK YOUTHS AND OTHERS FROM SUS
THEY DESERVE BETTER TREATMENT
SCRAP SUS NOW !!

"Suspected of loitering with intent"

BLACK PEOPLE'S ORGANISATIONS CAMPAIGN AGAINST SUS

Black people saw the need to fight the harassment of young blacks systematically by attacking special provisions like 'Sus' – which stated that, on the say of two policemen (and no evidence), anyone could be arrested as being about to commit an offence – and special squads like the Special Patrol Group (SPG) which saturated black areas for weeks stopping and searching anyone they suspected.

Sus

Organ of the Steering Committee
BPOCAS

Number 1 June 1978   Price 10p

Black Organisations Launch
CAMPAIGN AGAINST SUS

WEDNESDAY 1 February 1978 will remain a memorable day in the history of black people in Britain. It was on that day that the Black People's Organisations Campaign against Sus (BPOCAS) was formed, as an umbrella organisation for many black groups, and together with a number of other groups, Barristers and Solicitors, launched the sus campaign which publicly called for:

• 1 The repeal of Section 4 of the 1824 Vagrancy Act commonly known as sus, under which the police can arrest anybody as a suspected person loitering with intent to commit a felonious offence.

• 2 An independent inquiry into police-black relations.

Nearly 200 people were at the public meeting held at John Evelyn School, Deptford. SE8. Speakers included Alex Lyon, MP and Claudius Johnson black youth student. The campaign was initiated by the West Indian-African Community Association whose members were concerned about the oppressive nature of the legislation, the repressive manner in which the police are using it and the depressive environment of the black community generally.

Below are extracts from speeches made at the meeting by Paul Boateng of the Paddington Law Centre and the Reverend Basil Manning of the North Lewisham Project. The first speaks of police repress in and how to fight it, the second of psychological effects of arrest on black youths and the concern of the black community.

Paul Boateng

"It is right that this campaign should be conducted ... repealing the Vagrancy Act that we in ... at contact with people like Alex Lyon, and that we should be aware of what political muscle we have to alter the Act but we must not forget that even if the Act is gone the problem of the police is there.

"Sus exists as an end of sus what we have to face within our own communities at the same time as supporting this campaign and fighting for the repeal of this Act is how we are going to cope with the problem of the police, how we are going to organise

ourselves to defend our youths, how we are going to react as a community when our youths are harassed, beaten and are picked up in the streets.

"We as people in court, as a community, how to come together and how to fight these cases I hope that you will give some time to discussing this Act this evening because we have two inter-distinguished black members of the Ba here, Ron Rose and Rudy Narayan who time and time again have been in the front line defending black youths, who have put the reputation of their careers on the line for our black people. It is very important that we know how to organise our defences how to organise our communities to give our youths support, and to show the

and a feeling of despair in the minds of some youngsters who, in fact, may end up as criminals."

"I remember counseling a 16-year-old boy from a local school sometime last year and do you know the thing he was most interested in was detention centre and how he could get in there and what it was like It had become a cult in his mind because of his daily experiences of what was happening to him and his mates. Or a 16-year-old who would say to me 'What are you on about Basil?' How can you tell me that it is not a place to do this or that or how can you tell me that we must try and change things when even if I do absolutely nothing time and again they will pick me up for nothing I might as well do something, in order that they can pick me up for something. This is a point which you may remember and I am just echoing. This is the one law where it seems to me that you are guilty unless proved innocent. You are guilty because you are black, in many cases and the disproportion amongst the number of people who are picked up on sus are in fact black.

"I have no illusions about the black community's response to the question of crime. I think our response is clear. And when I have spoken to parents and the West Indian-African Community Association time and time again they have said 'if our children have in fact committed an offence then the police are here to do a particular job'. That is what the people of the black community are saying. But we do take exception to the fact that ... me and again our youngsters are being picked up for an offence is nothing.

"But that is not happening at in the black community. It seems to me that it is happening in a context of discrimination and of discrimination. This is the same in I am told by historians in another era of depression used then to pick up people and it was used again on heads in the 60s. It seems to me now in a time of high unemployment and with all the deprivation in the inner cities that it is being used against the black community."

police that no ... mind the wishes of this attack on communities we are not going to lie down and be mucked.

"The other thing which is brought up by the police when representations have been made in our Association that they expect the situation to rise because of pre-occ a crime it is their job preventative work. As some people have already said in this room seem that most of doing preventative work with even more ... wat their teething in that class

Mark Rusher/IFL

To win over public opinion, police and press orchestrated a campaign against a new 'crime' – mugging – a crime for which a 16-year-old boy received a 20-year sentence in 1972. In 1975, Lewisham police called in the SPG after first releasing to the press figures of 'black muggings'. The National Front picked up the theme, marching through the Borough in protest. Soon after, twenty-one young black people in Lewisham were charged with conspiracy to rob.

Boy of 16 gets 20 years for mugging

By ROSEMARY COLLINS

A boy aged 16 who was said to be the ringleader in a mugging was ordered to be detained for 20 years by Birmingham Crown Court yesterday. His two 15-year-old companions were ordered to be detained for 10 years. Mr Justice Croom-Johnson described it as "a serious and horrible case."

Paul Storey (16), of Villa Road, Handsworth, had admitted to charges of attempted murder and robbery. Mustafa Fuat and James Joseph Duignan, both 15, of Terrace Road and Churchill Road, Handsworth, had admitted wounding with intent to cause grievous bodily harm.

The charges arose from a "mugging" which took place in Villa Road on November 5. The boys admitted asking a man for a cigarette and knocking him to the ground while his attention was distracted.

After passing sentence Mr Justice Croom-Johnson asked that the three he brought back before him tomorrow. He gave no reason for the recall.

Mr Patrick Bennett, QC, prosecuting, claimed that they then dragged the man, Mr Robert Keegan, aged 31, to waste ground near by, that Paul Storey hit him again with a hunk and that the other two boys kicked him as he lay upon the ground. Mr Keegan, it was said, might suffer permanent behaviour changes and some loss in intellectual capacity because of the attack.

Duignan and Storey, who admitted taking the cigarettes, a bunch of keys and dog from Mr Keegan, called an ambulance and at first claimed they they

had found the man lying injured. Later Duignan and Fuat went to the police because they said that the matter was weighing on their consciences and that the mugging had started as "a bit of fun."

It was as a result of Duignan and Fuat's information that Paul Storey was arrested. Duignan had absconded from approved school at the time of the attack.

The length of the sentences provoked a local outcry in Handsworth. The Villa Road area is one where the police do not enjoy a good relationship with the large immigrant community, and where teenage unemployment is high.

A social worker who knows Paul Storey said that he was the oldest of three sons of an English mother, but that he had never known his West Indian father. He had been in minor trouble before, and was fined £10 last May for committing a disorderly act. Since leaving school he had been

Mr Justice Croom-Johnson

Violence on the dole
Murder-and-mugger land

Killing No 20 hits borough where violence is a way of life

COLOURED YOUTHS BLAMED FOR 80pc OF LOCAL MUGGING

Yard squad moves in to clear up mugging

EXTRA POLICE HELP TO HALVE MUGGINGS

Blacks get blame

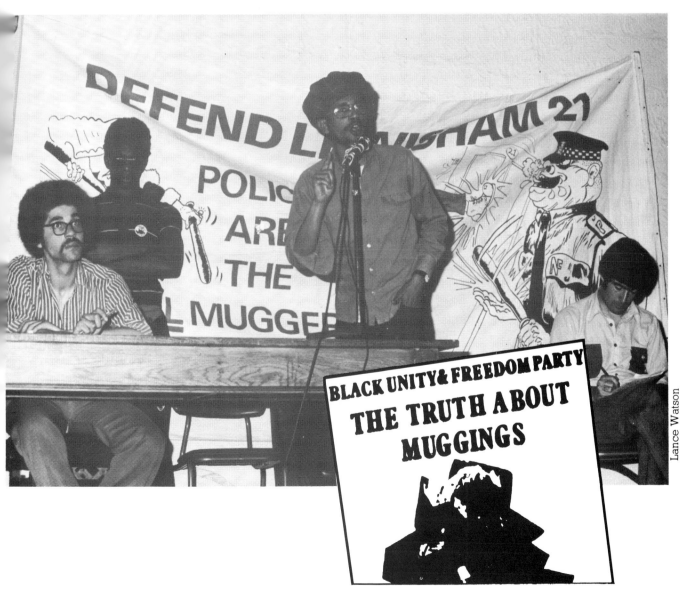

Black deaths in police custody and prison

1971: Aseta Simms died in police custody. The police doctor noted that she was bruised and her brain swollen, but could not determine the cause of death. Police alleged she was drunk and had brought about her own death.

1971: Andre Savvas died in police custody. He was arrested and taken to Hornsey police station. He had a fractured skull. The police are alleged to have commented on his abnormally thin skull.

1972: David Oluwale's body was dragged from a river in Leeds. Two Leeds policemen were charged with his manslaughter.

1974: Stephen Bernard was taken to a local police station after his relatives phoned for an ambulance. He was held at the police station and later charged with damaging it. In court he was discharged and recommended for admittance to hospital. The following morning he died.

1974: John Lamaletie died days after his wife had seen him being forcibly held by police and punched on both sides of his neck. Afterwards he complained of headaches but was advised not to make a complaint against the police. Cause of death was a blood clot in the artery by having the artery constricted.

1977: Adeenarain Neelayya died in police custody. Police alleged he was drugged or drunk on arrest and fit enough to be detained. He was found dead in his cell within an hour.

1979: S. Singh Grewal died after being held in Southall police station for two and a half hours. Police say he died from inhalation of his vomit. His family and doctor were not allowed to see his body for nine days.

1979: Two Nigerians were found dead — one at West End police station, the other in Brixton Prison. Both were alleged to have committed suicide.

1979: John Eshiett died in police custody after being arrested and charged with the murder of his common law wife.

1979: Henry Floyd died from asphyxia due to hanging.

1981: Pratap Lakha Sisodia died in a police cell in Surrey.

1981: Winston Rose died in a police van as he was being taken unconscious and vomiting to a police station.

1981: Richard Cartoon Campbell was found dead at Ashford Remand Centre after he had been heavily drugged. An independent inquiry placed responsibility on the Centre for his death.

1981: Shafique Míah died in police custody in Birmingham.

1982: Paul Worrell was found dead in his cell three days before his release date from Brixton prison. He had been arrested after reporting an incident during which he had been racially taunted.

1982: Thomas Connor died in Brixton police station.

1982: 70-year-old John Sugue died in Brixton police station. The post-mortem gave the cause of death as broncho-pneumonia due to cerebral contusions (bruises to the head).

1982: Simeon Collins died as a result of injuries to his liver and spleen after being arrested for being drunk and incapable.

1983: James Ruddock, described as a vagrant with a history of mental illness, diabetes and sickle cell anaemia, died in police custody.

1983: Nicholas Ofusu died after been taken to Rotherhithe police station and was reported to have suffocated on inhaling his own vomit.

1983: David McKay died in Brixton prison.

1983: Stephen Bowley hanged himself at the Borstal in Strangeways prison, Manchester, three days after being sentenced for attempted robbery and theft.

1983: Colin Roach died from a shotgun blast in the foyer of Stoke Newington police station, North London.

1983: Matthew Paul died in police custody at Leman police station after being kept incommunicado for two days.

1984: Michael Dean Martin was arrested after being racially taunted. He was transferred to a special hospital for the criminally insane although he did not have a criminal record and had never been in trouble with the police. He is alleged to have choked to death on his own vomit.

1985: Rush I (Harold Roberts) was taken to Prestwich mental hospital after he refused to acknowledge the magistrates court. He was found hanged.

1985: John Mikkleson, a Hells Angel, died after he was beaten while being taken into police custody.

No death in police custody has been allowed to go unchallenged.

The Tory Immigration Act and Industrial Relations Act of 1971 threatened to keep the black working class permanently at the bottom.

Hyde Park mass protest against the Immigration Bill, London, 1971.

Demonstration called by the Campaign Against Racist Laws, 1983.

As blacks, they were subjected to the threat of deportation...

Demonstration against deportations, Manchester, 1981.

As workers, fighting wretched pay and conditions, they had little help from the trade union movement which, because of new industrial relations legislation, was even more reluctant to take up black workers' causes.

THE RACE STRIKE AT S.T.C.

'IT'S RACIAL VICTIMISATION'

SAY BLACK WORKERS ON STRIKE

Violence flared up on the picket lines of the race strike at the Standard Telephones and Cables (S.T.C.) factory at New Southgate. A van tried to run over pickets twice and even police officers narrowly escaped injury. Angry black workers smashed the windscreen of the van and rained bottles and bricks.

In another incident eight carloads of National Front men approached the factory gates and attempted to intimidate the black workers on strike. The strike has gone on for over five weeks over a racial dispute where white machine setters are refusing to train black workers for skilled jobs. (Full story below).

RACE STRIKE

Telephones and Cables factory, New Southgate, London N.11 is the scene of a five-week strike by workers against an attempt by workers and the management of a South African style apartheid factory. Even though the strike is declared official by the union which the black workers belong to, UWC only one white worker, a shop stewards convenor, has come to support. All the white workers shop stewards are at work and a majority of black workers in protest against the racial victimisation of a fellow worker.

Standard Telephones and Cables, who manufacture telephone equipment and components, employ about 8,000 people. It is a subsidiary of the giant I.T.T. (International Telephone and Cables) who has vast interests in Chile and South Africa and is frequently involved in plots to topple Third World governments. Their factory at New Southgate employs 5,000 people. About 1,000 are in the machine shop where the work employs setters (skilled men to set the machines) and operators to run the machines. All the setters are white and the majority of the operators are black.

The setters who earn around £32 are trained from the ranks of operators whose jobs are dull, hard and monotonous (like drilling in a small piece of wood 6,000 times a day

Until 1969 all the shop stewards were white, who made sure that only white workers were promoted to the job of setter. There are many black workers who have been employed there for 20 years or more and are still operators. The black workers protested and managed to get their own shop stewards elected, whereupon all the white setters left the union AEUW and joined ETU, the electricians' union that has always advocated strong immigration controls.

BRO. ADAMS

The machine shop works round the clock. The night shift employing 120 workers is almost entirely black and the day shift employing about 300 is 95% black. After an 18 month struggle involving numerous stoppages and go slows the management and the white setters' union agreed to train

one black worker. For this the setters were given £1.50 a week extra for training Brother Roderick Adams, a black operator in the night shift, was selected and started training in December 1972. He had been training for eight months when on 16 July he was informed that the white setters' union ETU had issued instructions that his training was to cease.

What happened was that two other vacancies for the job of setter had occurred in the day shift. The management and the white shop stewards got together and tried to fill in the jobs with white operators who had been there only a few months. The black shop stewards found this out and protested. One job was filled by an Irishman who had only been there for six months and who cannot read properly and has bad eyesight. But the other

cont. on p. 2

Black workers occupy factory in wages battle

Engineering workers from Stanmore Engineering Works at Alperton have been occupying their factory for nearly five weeks.

The occupation is in support of the national wage claim of the Amalgamated Engineering and Foundry Workers (AUEW). Their demands are:

1. £6 weekly increase
2. 35-hour working
3. 4 weeks annual
4. Holiday pay basings.
5. Wages for lay-

tory made over £½ a million profit last year and they tell us they haven't got any money. We are on basic earnings of £17 per week."

Brother Linton criticised the leadership of the AUEW "Scanlon & Company didn't

BLACK VOICE
POPULAR PAPER OF
THE BLACK UNITY & FREEDOM PARTY
VOL 3   NO 3   1972   PRICE 5P

This left black workers to fight alone against the racism of management and scabbing by the white workforce. Black strike committees went from factory to factory – from Mansfield Hosiery, Standard Telephones and Cables, Stanmore Engineering, Harwood Cash, Imperial Typewriters – giving support and advice.

John Sturrock/Report

HERE TO STAY; HERE TO FIGHT

HARAMBEE V. THE THIEVES

Brother Herman addresses an Institute of Race Relations meeting

On Wednesday July 26, four bailiffs with two policemen entered 37 Cowper Road N16. They broke down three doors, appropriated books, records, typewriters and chairs — in lieu of rates owing on the premises.

The amount of debt? £115.

The occupants of the premises? Harambee — a 'rehabilitation' project which educates, trains, houses and generally cares for black youth — run by Brother Herman.

This was merely one in a series of 'state' attacks mounted against Brother Herman and Harambee over the last two years — attacks which have increased in viciousness and pettiness as Bro. Herman has resolutely refused to 'be bought'.

Two weeks later Herman was sentenced to 60 days in prison for failing to pay a fine of £120, imposed after a charge under the Noise Abatement Act following a fund-raising party last March. And, once out of jail, Herman was threatened by a visit of Scotland Yard who wished to examine his books.

Between 1973/4 some £3,000,000 was given to black community projects as part of the government's strategy of containing the black community and defusing its political potential.

Some found its way to bona fide black projects like Harambee, which is about ten years old. A quarter of a million was allocated as a capital grant and £55,000 per annum to meet running costs. Of the capital grant Bro. Herman has received £6,000 (over four years). Of the running costs he had £39,000 in one year, £26,000 the next, and none since.

Colonial mentality

One year after the monies had first been disbursed, the Islington Council began to impose impossible conditions. They wanted to inspect the accounts **at any time**, they wanted the title deeds on all the properties Harambee owned (ie those purchased without their money) and so on.

The colonial mentality was back with a vengeance according to Herman — blacks were not ready for true independence, for governing their own affairs.

"These guys, as we say in the West Indies, they want to BE IN CHARGE, and, if they can't be in charge of one nigger..."

Though other projects caved in to the cond... Islington, He... intimidated... sophy based... teaching of... that "Black... strong so as... racism. No c... to build our:

He also k... Council an... jealous of i...

Now the youth, many of whom were born in Britain, became the focus of the state's attention. Millions of pounds were pumped into black self-help groups to destroy their independence and stamp out the breeding ground of resistance.

And it failed.

Groups like the Harambee project refused to accept the strings attached to state handouts; its leader went to jail.

Black Defiance

Long robes?
Grey wig?
Disguise yourself little man
But we know who you are.
If in the light of day
You hide your face
How can you be trusted in the dark?
Little man, you may disguise yourself
And exaggerate your twisted sense of self-importance
While basking in the security
Of a tyrannical power made legal by tradition
But we are watching you
We know who you are.

How do we plead you ask
We refuse to participate in rituals
That sanctify hypocrisy
And legitimise injustice.

How do we plead you ask
We have been pleading for centuries
We plead no more
Clenched fist salutes
And Black defiance is our reply.

SPAGHETTI: THE SIX LONG DAYS

A. Munroe   F. Davies   W. Dick

THE TRIAL OF brothers Frank Davis, Wesley Dick and Anthony Munroe started on June 8, amid dramatic scenes in which black defendants for the first time in British history refused to recognise the court.

IN ABSENCE

When asked to plead, he stated that black people have been pleading for too long and turned their backs on the Judge. When prison officers forced them round, two of the defendants took out banners from under their shirts, one of which read "Bury Fascism", while Anthony Munroe started to read a prepared statement.

The presiding Judge Mervyn Griffith-Jones, known to be one of the harshest judges at the old Bailey, immediately sent them down to the cells. The trial continued in their absence. The judge said to the jury that it was an ordinary criminal trial but that the defendants had started to make a "Black Power" demonstration. Eighteen jurors were challenged and the final jury includes only two black men and one white woman.

The court heard how the brothers were trapped by police after one of the managers had escaped in the initial minutes of the raid and raised the alarm. When armed police officers arrived within two minutes, the brothers and their hostages retreated to the storeroom where they remained for five days, 22 hours and seven minutes.

The conversation there went as follows:

The police investigations were helped when one of Rondel's accomplices, George Kyriades went to Knightsbridge and made a series of statements that enabled them to arrest Rondel, the alleged getaway car driver, brother Addison, and the informant who pleaded guilty, Lilo Termine. Giuseppe Serano, one of the hostages, was not called as a prosecution witness, appearing instead for the defence.

There were revelations of a sophisticated laser camera and recording equipment that was lowered through holes made in the ceiling.

POLICE: We are armed police officers. Come out with your hands up

BROTHERS: We are too, copper.

POLICE: What arms have you got?

VOICE: (laughter) we have 50 machine guns, tanks, hand red grenade launchers, rockets.

POLICE: What group do you represent?

VOICE: We are members of the Black Liberation Army. I am Franklin Peter Davies, born Nigeria.

POLICE: What are the names of your companions?

VOICE: You must be joking.

The brothers again stated that they constituted a call of the Black Liberation Army and demanded the release of the Brockwell Three and the dropping of all charges against the Cricklewood 11. When no response came from the police, their demands were amended to a minibus to take them to the airport and a plane to take them to an undisclosed destination in return for the release of their hostages.

In September 1975, three Afro-Caribbean youths, in the hope of financing black self-help groups, held up a Knightsbridge Spaghetti House.

Shujaa Moshesh (formerly Wesley Dick) still serving his sentence in 1986.

At the Notting Hill carnival of 1976, black youth finally exploded into direct confrontation with the police.

The newspaper clipping headline reads:

POWELL WARNS MPs: RACIAL CONFLICT COULD MAKE BELFAST SEEM AN ENVIABLE PLACE

Angry scenes in debate on immigration

THE SUN

SCANDAL OF £600-A-WEEK IMMIGRANTS

Giant bill for two families who live in a

Among Asians too, it was the youth who were moving into the forefront of struggle. Fascist attacks were mounting and police provided no protection.

In May 1976, (as in 1968), the press and politicians were giving prominence to Powell and his claims of a government cover-up on immigration. The effect on the streets was immediate.

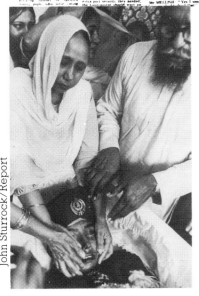

John Sturrock/Report

Chris Davies/Network

On June 4, Gurdip Singh Chaggar was stabbed to death by a white youth in the heart of Southall. The Asian youth marched to the police station demanding redress and refused to move. The next day Southall Youth Movement was born.

Mike Abrahams/Network

Here to stay . . . / 33

Racist attacks all over the country always provoked reaction.

Mass demonstration in East London after the murder of Akhtar Ali Baig, 1980.

Youth movements in Bradford, Brick Lane, Newham and Hackney arose to meet the fascist onslaught.

Defending communities from attack brought the youth into confrontation with the police...

in Leicester

...Tottenham

Carlos Augusto/IFL

...Southall

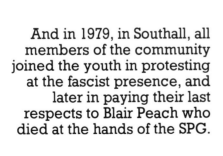

And in 1979, in Southall, all members of the community joined the youth in protesting at the fascist presence, and later in paying their last respects to Blair Peach who died at the hands of the SPG.

Unsupported by press or politicians and unprotected by the police, youth groups turned to self-defence – and then had to prove in the courts that 'Self Defence was No Offence'.

VICTIMS OF RACIAL ATTACK AND INJUSTICE

AT STAKE - THE RIGHT OF ASIAN PEOPLE TO DEFEND THEMSELVES

On 19 July 1978, Judge Michael Argyle of the Old Bailey sentenced:
JOGINDER SINGH VIRK (24) to 7 years imprisonment;
MOHINDER SINGH VIRK (27) to 3 years;
BALVINDER SINGH VIRK (21) to 2 years;
SUKHVINDER SINGH VIRK (18: a student) to 3 months.

THEIR CRIME?
    a) Not to tolerate racial abuses, insults and physical assaults in front of their house by the racist white youths
    b) To fight back in self-defence
    c) To seek police protection
    d) And above all to have a black skin

WHAT HAPPENED?
    * They were repairing their car in front of their home when a gang of 5 white youths shouted racial abuses and attacked them. They had to defend themselves. They called the police for their protection.
    * The police let the attackers go free.
    * The defenders were arrested, charged with causing grievous bodily harm and they were refused bail for two days.
    * They were treated as confirmed criminals and made to report at the police station every day for 18 months. Their passports were also taken.
    * A student of 16, charged only with threatening behaviour to a policeman's witness, was not spared from reporting daily.
    * In the racial fight no Asians were called as witnesses despite the fact that some people knew something about the incident.

RELEASE THE VIRKS

The Virk brothers, victims of a white racist attack, defended themselves and were then given very heavy sentences in the courts.

John Smith/IFL

Twelve Asian youths protecting their community from racist attacks were charged with conspiracy to cause explosions after petrol bombs were found.

Eight Newham school boys who resisted an attack from plain-clothes policemen, believing them to be fascists, were charged with assault.

David Hoffman

BLACK WOMEN

The racist climate of Thatcher's Britain cut into the very fabric of black life. And, as before, threw up a new leadership – this time the black women's movement.

By the mid-1970s, black women, weary of male sexism and feminist racism, began to form groups all over the country, as well as a powerful national body. Through OWAAD, Asian and Afro-Caribbean experiences could cross-fertilise and develop lines of struggle that would benefit the whole community.

Claudia Jones

Women like Claudia Jones and Mrs Amy Ashwood Garvey had already taken up women's issues in the 1940s and 1950s.

Amy Ashwood Garvey

In the Black Power movement and the industrial strikes women had always been involved.

Strike at Kenilworth Components Factory, 1974

Laurie Sparham/Network

Women saw that racism now affected every aspect of black life. They added their own perspectives on black prisoners, on health and on surveillance.

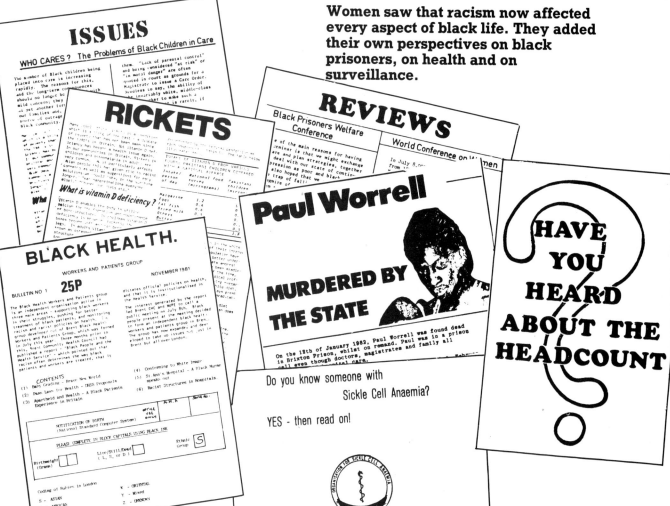

Women brought new dimensions to old issues –

when Asians entering Britain were subjected to 'virginity tests';

HM IMMIGRATION OFFICE
Terminal 3 London (Heathrow) Airport Hounslow
Middlesex TW6 1ND

Telephone 01-897 9691 ext

Your reference

Our reference

Date 24.1.79

This is to certify that I Miss ████████ agree to a gynaecological examination which may be a vaginal if necessary.
This statement has been read to me in my own mother tongue and is fully understood by me.

Signed

Witnessed ～～～   S. RADIOGRAPHER.

and they joined and broadened existing campaigns, for example over deportations.

FAMILIES FIGHT TO BE UNITED

MANDA MUST STAY

STOP THE DEPORTATIONS!

After a two-year fight against deportation, Leyton resident Shahid Syed, his wife Nasreen and two-year-old daughter Sidrah, have been ordered to leave the country. Despite an appeal court hearing still pending, the Home Office has thrown out his plea to stay in this country, even though Nasreen has a chronic heart condition and requires regular medical treatment which she will be unable to receive in Pakistan. Legal advisers have assured Shahid that the Home Office cannot pre-empt the appeal court judgement by forcing the deportation to go ahead but unless the appeal court rules in his favour, the prospect of reversing the deportation order looks grim.

SHAHID SYED DEFENCE CAMPAIGN

Andrew Wiard/Report

Laurie Sparham/Network

Andrew Wiard/Report

Andrew Wiard/Report

Black women never forgot that they were part of the working class. They supported many women on strike. The Grunwick dispute of 1976/7, which was betrayed by the white unions, emphasised the need for self-organisation and self-reliance.

John Sturrock/Network

Laurie Sparham/Network

Black women, mothers to those being harassed on the streets and rail-roaded into jail, now led the campaigns against police brutality and increased police powers.

Demonstration outside Brixton police station, 1979.

Trafalgar Square rally against immigration laws, 1979.

Black People Against State Brutality march, London, 1979.

REBELLION

Daily doses of brutalising racism, a future of unemployment and social deprivation and an intense distrust and dislike of a police force which locked them into the ghetto, led inevitably to uprisings by the youth.

G.M. Cookson

" In April, Brixton exploded into rebellion, in July Southall — for blacks, Afro-Caribbean and Asian alike, all distinction between police and fascist had faded ... For the deprived of slum city — black and white — the state was the police."

(A. Sivanandan, 1981)

You wonder why we uprise

Politically unstabilised

Economically destabilised

People dehumanised

Youth criminalised

Mentally vandalised

Housing ghettoised

Politically unrecognised

And you wonder why we uprise.

Leroy Cooper, Liverpool 8.

In the heart of the ghetto, the police, press and politicians made a concerted attempt in the years after 1981 to divide Afro-Caribbeans from Asians.

After the 1985 uprising in Handsworth, in which two Asians lost their lives, the need to preserve black unity took on a new urgency. In a symbolic joint ceremony, black leaders laid wreaths outside the post office where the two had died.

Meanwhile, blacks, outraged by the shooting of
Cherry Groce in Brixton and the death of Cynthia
Jarrett in Tottenham, marched in their thousands
through London.

FURTHER READING

An asterisk (*) indicates easier texts

General
* Thomas J. Cottle, *Black testimony: voices of Britain's West Indians* (London, Wildwood House, 1978)
Ann Dummett, *A portrait of English racism* (London, Christians Against Racism and Fascism, 1984)
Paul Gordon, *White law: racism in the police, courts and prisons* (London, Pluto, 1983)
Chris Searle, *The Forsaken Lover: white words and black people* (London, Penguin, 1973)
A. Sivanandan, *A different hunger: writings on black resistance* (London, Pluto Press, 1982)

Introduction
Adolph Edwards, *Marcus Garvey 1887-1940* (London, New Beacon Books, 1967)
* Institute of Race Relations, *Roots of racism* (London, IRR, 1982)
* Institute of Race Relations, *Patterns of racism* (London, IRR, 1982)
* Krishna Kripalani, *Gandhi: a life* (New Delhi, National Book Trust, India, 1968)

Arrival, Organising self-reliance and Fighting discrimination
G.S. Aurora, *The new frontiersmen* (Bombay, Popular Prakashan, 1967)
* Beverley Bryan et al, *The heart of the race: black women's lives in Britain* (London, Virago, 1985)
* Campaign Against Racism and Fascism/Southall Rights, *Southall: the birth of a black community* (London, Institute of Race Relations, 1981), Chapters 1, 2 and 3
* Buchi Emecheta, *Second class citizen* (London, Allison & Busby, 1974), fiction
Peter Fryer, *Staying power: the history of black people in Britain* (London, Pluto, 1984), Chapters 9, 10, 11
Donald Hinds, *Journey to an illusion* (London, Heinemann, 1966)
Derek Humphry and Gus John, *Because they're black* (Harmondsworth, Penguin, 1972)
* Institute of Race Relations, *How racism came to Britain* (London, IRR, 1985)
Buzz Johnson, *'I think of my mother': notes on the life and times of Claudia Jones* (London, Karia, 1985)
George Lamming, *The emigrants* (London, Allison & Busby, 1980), fiction
Peter Marsh, *Anatomy of a strike* (London, Institute of Race Relations, 1967)
Stephen B. Oates, *Let the trumpet sound: the life of Martin Luther King Junior* (London, Search Press, 1982)
Ron Ramdin, *The making of the black working class in Britain* (Farnborough, Gower, 1986)
E. Scobie, *Black Britannia: a history of blacks in Britain* (Chicago, Johnson, 1972), Part 2
A. Sivanandan, *From resistance to rebellion: Asian and Afro-Caribbean struggles in Britain* (London, IRR, 1986)

Film
Riots and rumours of riots by Imruh Caesar, 1981 §

Black Power
Stokely Carmichael and Charles V. Hamilton, *Black Power* (Harmondsworth, Penguin, 1969)
Frantz Fanon, *Black skin white masks* (London, Pluto, 1986)
Malcolm X, *The Autobiography of Malcolm X* (Harmondsworth, Penguin, 1966)
A. Sivanandan, 'Black power: the politics of existence' in *A different hunger*
Times News Team, *The black man in search of power* (London, Nelson 1968)

Forging black unity
Amilcar Cabral, *Return to the source* (London, Monthly Review, 1973)
Angela Davis, *If they come in the morning* (London, Orbach & Chambers, 1971)

Paul Foot, *The rise of Enoch Powell* (Harmondsworth, Penguin, 1969)
Walter Rodney, *How Europe underdeveloped Africa* (London, Bogle l'Ouverture, 1972)
Walter Rodney, *The groundings with my brothers* (London, Bogle l'Ouverture, 1969)

Building black community
Battersea and Wandsworth Trades Council, *The death of Richard 'Cartoon' Campbell* (London, nd)
* Campaign Against Racism and Fascism/Southall Rights, *Southall: the birth of a black community* (London, Institute of Race Relations, 1981)
Bernard Coard, *How the West Indian child is made educationally sub-normal in the British school system* (London, New Beacon, 1971)
* Zeynep Hasbudak and Brian Simons, *Zeynep: that really happened to me* (London, ALTARF, 1986)
Institute of Race Relations, *Police against black people* (London, IRR, 1979)
* Robert Moore, *Racism and black resistance in Britain* (London, Pluto, 1975)
A. Sivanandan, *From resistance to rebellion*

Here to stay, Here to fight
The Black liberator (No. 1, December 1978)
Blood on the streets: a report ... on racial attacks in East London (London, Bethnal Green and Stepney Trades Council, 1978)
* Campaign against racism and fascism/Southall Rights, *Southall: the birth of a black community* (London, IRR, 1981)
* Tariq Mehmood, *Hand on the sun* (Harmondsworth, Penguin, 1983), fiction
National Council for Civil Liberties, *Southall 23 April 1979* (London, NCCL, 1980)
A. Sivanandan, 'Race, class and the state' in *A different hunger*

Films
Blacks Brittanica, directed by David Koff and Musindo Mwinyipembe, 1978 §
Blood Ah go run, directed by Kuumba Black Arts, 1982 §
Struggles for black community, 4 films by Race & Class Ltd, directed by Colin Prescod, 1981 §
  – A common history (Leicester)
  – From you were black you were out (Notting Hill)
  – Tiger Bay is my home (Cardiff)
  – A town under siege (Southall)

Black women
Black Workers Support Group, *Black struggles in Brent* (London, BWSG, nd)
* *Breaking the silence: writing by Asian women*, (London, Centerprise, 1984)
* Beverley Bryan et al, *The heart of the race*
* Campaign against racism and fascism/Southall Rights, *Southall: the birth of a black community*, Chapter 2
* Elyse Dodgson, *Motherland: West Indian women to Britain in the 1950s* (London, Heinemann, 1984)
* Amrit Wilson, *Finding a voice: Asian women in Britain* (London, Virago, 1978), Chapter 3

Rebellion
A different reality: an account of black people's experiences and their grievances before and after the Handsworth rebellion of September 1985 (Birmingham, West Midlands County Council, 1986)
The Broadwater Farm inquiry: report of the independent inquiry into disturbances of October 1985 at the Broadwater Farm Estate, Tottenham (London, 1986)
Institute of Race Relations, *Rebellion and repression* (Special issue of *Race & Class*, Autumn 1981/Winter 1982)
* Tariq Mehmood, *Hand on the sun*

Films
The people's account, directed by Milton Bryan, 1986, distributed by Ceddo
Struggles for black community, 4 films by Race & Class Ltd

§ Distributed by The Other Cinema, 79 Wardour Street, London W1